A PICTORIAL HISTORY OF
AMERICAN GOLF

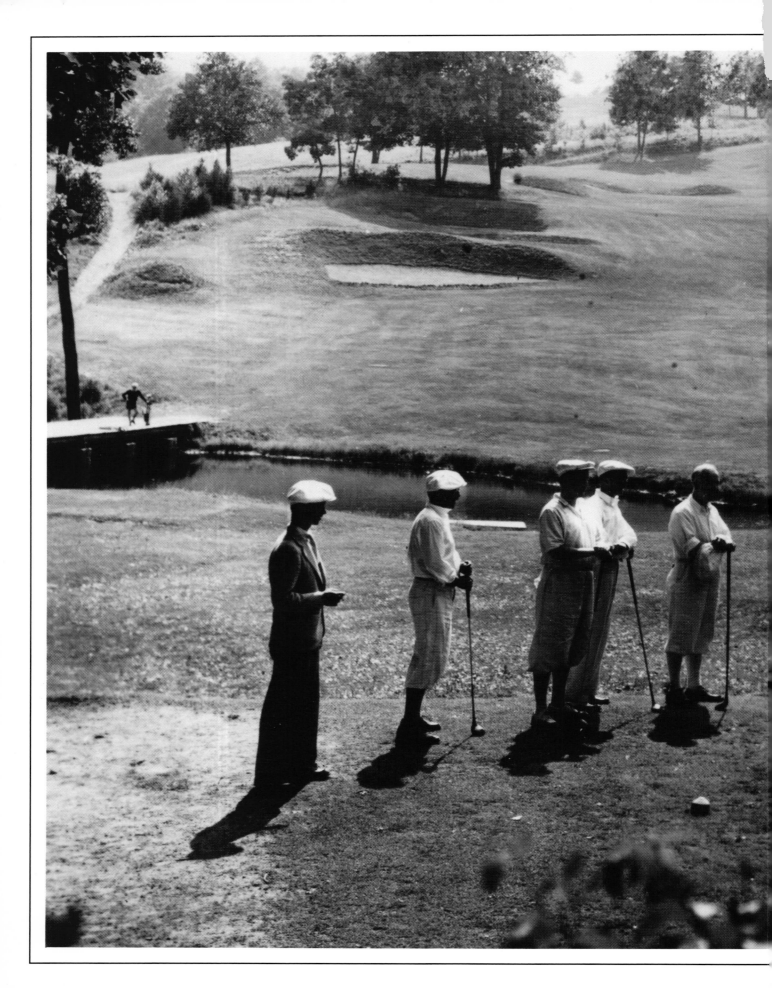

A Pictorial History Of American Golf

To William Wallace Petrie, 1914-1965

Special thanks to the United States Library of Congress, whose vast pictorial archives made this book possible. Thanks also to the *New York Times'* faithful chronicle of the grand game from arrival on our shores to the present day.

WILLOW CREEK PRESS
P.O. Box 147 • Minocqua, WI 54548

ISBN 1-57223-145-9
Printed in Canada

TABLE OF CONTENTS

HUMBLE BEGINNINGS

2. *The first photograph of golf in America.*

HUMBLE BEGINNINGS

THE FIRST CODE OF GOLF RULES (1745)

I. You must Tee your Ball within a Club length of the Hole.

II. Your Tee must be upon the ground.

III. You are not to change the Ball which you strike off the Tee.

IV. You are not to remove Stones, Bones, or any Break-club for the sake of playing your Ball, except upon the fair Green, and that only within a Club length of your Ball.

V. If your Ball come among Water, or any watery filth, you are at liberty to take out your Ball, and bringing it behind the hazard, and teeing it, you may play it with any club and allow your Adversary a stroke for so getting out your Ball.

VI. If your Balls be found anywhere touching one another, you are to lift the first Ball till you play the last.

VII. At holing, you are to play your ball honestly for the Hole, and not play upon your Adversary's Ball, not lying in your way to the Hole.

XII. He whose Ball lies farthest from the Hole is obliged to play first.

VIII. If you should lose your Ball by its being taken up, or in any other way, you are to go back to the spot where you struck last, and drop another Ball, and allow your Adversary a stroke for the misfortune.

IX. No man, at Holing his ball, is to be allowed to mark to the Hole with his Club or anything else.

X. If a ball be stop'd by any person, Horse, Dog, or anything else, the Ball so stop'd must be played where it lies.

XI. If you draw your Club in order to strike, and proceed as far in the stroke as to bringing down your Club – if then your Club shall break in any way, it is to be accounted a stroke.

XIII. Neither Trench, Ditch, nor Dyke made for the preservation of the Links, nor the Scholars' holes, nor the Soldiers' lines, shall be accounted a Hazard, but the Ball is to be taken out, Teed, and played with any iron Club.

– Adapted by the Royal and Ancient Golf Club,
 of St. Andrews (Scotland) and the St. Andrew's
 Golf Club of Yonkers, New York, 1888.

---

1. *Americans owe a perpetual debt of gratitude to the Scots who essentially invented the grand game, defined the rules of play and initially lead the way in developing courses and equipment.* 2. *Golf came to America in 1888 when John Reid received a gift of Scottish golf clubs and two dozen gutta-percha balls. Shortly thereafter, Reid and several friends laid out an informal three-hole course in a pasture across the street from his Yonkers home. That historic first round of golf in America was chronicled photographically. The players, pictured from left, are Harry Holbrook, Alexander Kinnan, John B. Upham and John Reid - unanimously deemed "The Father of American Golf". Holbrook's sons served as caddies. The players, inspired by both the personal and competitive challenges of the unique game, later repaired to Reid's home to form the St. Andrew's Golf Club.*

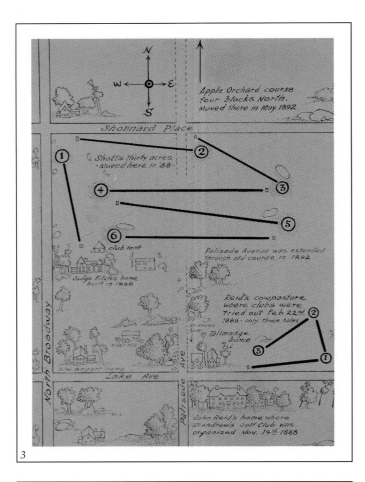

3, 4, 5. Although ridiculed publicly and privately for their keen interest in an apparently silly game, St. Andrew's players not only persisted, they flourished and multiplied. By 1892, St. Andrew's relocated to a nearby apple orchard. The thirteen members became known as "The Apple Tree Gang" not for the course's general landscape, but for a specific tree around which the men gathered after their rounds to congratulate or commiserate one another with "refreshments". The apple tree, of course, became America's first nineteenth hole.

6. An 1892 instructional sequence illustrating the ungainly style of the era.

BON TON GOLF

"As soon as the game was over all hands adjourned to the clubhouse for tea and gossip and to discuss in particular the popular new creation — the golfing cloak. The next day the men were permitted to hold a tournament, and they bettered substantially the remarkable low scores made by the women golfers."

–The New York Sun, 1894, reporting on the first women's tournament held in Morristown, New Jersey.

AN ELITIST GAME?

Society is as prone to fads as are the sparks to fly upward. And the latest in outdoor fads is golf. Tennis, archery and polo have each had their turn, and golf is now coming in to replace them in the fickle minds of the Four Hundred.

Without being as violent as tennis or polo, the ancient Scottish game furnishes more exercise than either archery or croquet and seems to find favor with those lovers of outdoor sports who are too stout, too old or too lazy to enjoy any of the severer games.

– New York Times, 1894

OR THE SPORT OF AN ENTIRE NATION?

In the history of American field sports there can be found no outdoor pastime that developed and attained such popularity in such a relatively short period of time as the game of golf.

–New York Times, 1895

PRESIDENTIAL TRIBUTE

When I learn that your club – the oldest in the country – is only twenty years old, and realize that I have been playing golf since 1896, I am surprised. I would, in respect to any other matter, feel very much discouraged at having attained in so long a time so little excellence. But golf is different from other games. Pope's lines have a greater application to it than to any other sport I know: "Hope springs eternal in the human breast; Man never is, but always will be, blest"

– President Taft, from a 1908 speech honoring the 20th anniversary of the St. Andrews Club.

AND YOU CALL THIS FUN?

Given a strong pair of lungs, firm muscles upon the legs and a healthy desire to emulate others in physical exercise, a man may become a golf player. Without these he had better stay out of the sport, for no man who cannot run several miles without stopping can make any kind of a respectable appearance in the game.

In addition to the fact that it appeals to men of athletic development, it is also by the nature of the game itself, a most aristocratic exercise; for no man can play at golf who

7. *President Taft, whose girth seemed to restrict proper follow-through, lifts one off the fairway in 1909. The President's hearty advocacy of the game did much to spread nationwide enthusiasm for golf.*

8. *The first green at St. Andrew's Grey Oaks course of 1894 was guarded by a steep bunker and flanked by a stone wall.*

has not a servant at command to assist him. The truth is that the servant is as essential to the success of the game as the player himself. Perhaps the best description of the game, which would certainly be unique in a republic, may be given in the words of one of the most expert players in this vicinity, Mr. Alexander D. MacFarlane.

To play golf properly we need a very large expanse of uncultivated soil. The first thing necessary is to dig a small hole perhaps one foot or two feet deep and about four inches in diameter. Beginning with this hole, a circle is devised that includes substantially the whole of the links. About once in 500 yards of this circle a hole is dug corresponding to the one I have just described. The design is to make as large a circle as possible, with holes at about the same distance apart.

The game then may be played, with two or four persons. If by four, two of them must be upon the same side. There are eleven implements of the game, most important of which is the ball. This is made of gutta-percha and is painted white. It weighs about two ounces and is just small enough to fit comfortably into the holes dug in the ground. Still it should not be so large that it cannot be taken out with ease. The other ten implements are the tools of the players. They are of various shapes as may be inferred from the names of the implements. The spoon, for instance, is a rough approximation to what we generally understand as a spoon and is designed to lift the ball out of holes, or sinks in the ground. The club, of course, is simply an instrument with which to bat the ball. The same practically applies to the driving putter. All these implements of the game are designed to fit into the various situations in which the player may find himself.

At the beginning of play, each player places his ball at the edge of a hole which has been designated as a starting point. When the word has been given to start, he bats his ball as accurately as possible toward the next hole, which may be, as I have said, either 100 or 500 yards distant. As soon as it is started in the air he runs forward in the direction which the ball has taken and his servant, who is called a "caddy", runs after him with all the other nine tools in his arms. If the player is expert or lucky, he bats his ball so that it falls within a few feet or inches, even, of the next hole in the circle. His purpose is to put the ball into the next hole, spoon it out and drive it forward to the next further one before his opponent can accomplish the same end. The province of the "caddy" in the game is to follow his master as closely as possible, generally at a dead run, and be ready to hand him whichever implement of the game the master calls for, as the play may demand. For instance, the ball may fall in such a way that it is lodged an inch or two above the ground, having fallen in thick grass. The player rushing up to it would naturally call upon his "caddy" for a baffing spoon and, having received it from the hands of his servant, he would bat the ball with the spoon in the direction of the next hole.

You can see that in this the "caddy" really gets about as much exercise out of the sport as his master, and he must be so familiar with the tools of the game that he can hand out the right implement at any moment when it is called for. If a player has succeeded in throwing or pushing his ball into a hole, his opponent must wait until he has succeeded in spooning it out before be begins to play. Obedience to this rule abviates any dispute as to the order in which a man's points are to be made. For if I have my ball in a hole and my opponent has his within an inch or two of it, he must wait before he plays until I have gotten my ball clear of it and thrown it towards the next hole. Following this general plan, the players go entirely about the circle, and, as you may see, in a large field it may involve a run of several miles. If I should throw my ball beyond the hole at which I must next enter, I am obliged to knock it back until it shall enter the desired place and be carefully spooned out again. While I am doing this, my opponent may, by a lucky play, get his ball within the proper limit and thus gain some distance on me.

– St. Louis Globe-Democrat, 1889, from a misinformed narrative describing the new game called "golf".

8

PROLIFERATION

1

2. Golf at DeLand, Florida, circa 1905.

PROLIFERATION

RITES OF SPRING

The golfing season is rapidly approaching and within the next month the game will be fairly under way in a score or more of enterprising clubs. Although a little early in the season, the links of many of the leading clubs have been put in first-class condition, and the more energetic devotees of the game have been busily engaged in getting back in their old-time playing trim again.

Among those who pursue golf, not so much for the social features which have been mingled with it, but from the stand-point of genuine science and solid playing, the game will be raised to a higher tone and dignity this season than it has ever before enjoyed in America. This is due to the successful organization of the United States Golf Association, which includes in its membership most of the prominent clubs in the country. This association will exercise a general supervision over the game throughout the country, its laws being accepted as the authority on the game in America, and it will take general charge of the championship matches. Thus the game is brought within the limits of definite organization, and as the leading clubs are represented on its Governing Board, all will have an interest in its success and in upholding its regulations.

– New York Times, April 1895

BRITISH GOLF HERO TO TOUR THE U.S.A.

Golfers may readily be excused for their enthusiasm over the arrival of Great Britain's open champion, Harry Vardon, if, indeed, anyone is disposed to cavil at them on that score, for Vardon is unmistakably the most brilliant golfer that has ever set foot upon American soil. The golfers are no more excited over the exponent of their game than have the followers of other sports been at various times over foreign visitors who have attained fame in their respective lines.

This is, moreover, the first time that an English championship holder has ever visited our shores. When Willie Park first came over about three years ago he was a former champion. For two years Vardon held the open championship of the United Kingdom, but by his victory last year he added a third championship triumph to his list of golf trophies, and it will be long before another golfer can come to America with a better or worthier record than Vardon possesses.

Those who remember Willie Park's coming and the ovation he received at every course he visited cannot be anything else than joyous at the prospect of seeing the ablest foreign golfer that has come here since that time. So far as outward appearances go, Vardon's arrival has been quieter than was Park's , but the enthusiasm is no

---

Although played only by the St. Andrew's members in 1888, golf had become the elitist activity of the Four Hundred by 1894. The compelling appeal of the game, however, refused to limit it to the upper classes and by 1905 America had become a nation of duffers with over a million participants and 2,000 courses.
1. Teeing off near Boise, Idaho, circa 1919.

less, and when milder weather causes the warm, blood of golfing ardor to flow more freely in the metropolitan district, matches may be arranged with even more rapidity than they were for Park. There may be this difference, however. Park came here to establish a golf club business, which has since been abandoned, and, while professional matches were arranged for him – notably the famous three-cornered one with Willie Dunn – Park gave exhibitions at several clubs freely. Vardon, on the other hand, is out for business as well as pleasure.

While one or two of our professionals might be bold enough to meet Vardon for a money purse, it is doubtful if many matches of that sort could be arranged. It is not at all likely that any professional would back himself very heavily, nor is it more certain that a professional would care to meet Vardon, knowing that the second man could not even see the color of the money.

Vardon is willing to play anyone who wishes to meet him, professional or amateur, or give any golfing exhibition that may be asked, but for these he is to be paid as any other performer would be. On the free basis Vardon would surely be overwhelmed with invitations, but even on the "pay-up" policy there will probably be

enough clubs ready to keep Vardon tolerably busy until he returns to England.

"It looks to me," remarked a Stock Exchange golfer, "as though the clubs that Vardon first visits would make money out of it. His fame has traveled so well ahead of him that every eager golfer is anxious to see him right off. When these men go to the club that has Vardon for the star attraction, they must all eat, surely smoke, and most all drink. They have to buy these things at the club. The club will have a first-class time, there will be plenty of sport and good-fellowship; it will give the club a few more inches of reputation, and I don't think its purse will be very empty toward the close of the day, even if $100 or $200 has been transferred to Vardon's pocket.

"What kind of a fellow is Vardon?" "How does he look?" have been the questions almost universally asked of those who have been among the first to meet the champion. The personal appearance of any hero is always interesting. It may be stated at once that Vardon carries none of the marks of his three championships on the exterior. Many a one-year amateur is far more pompous in his golfing talk and regalla than is Vardon. No one could be more modest than he. His frank, clear-cut face lights

3

Men, women, children – American golfers came in all shapes, sizes and, unfortunately to a lesser degree, colors.

3. "Driving from the ninth tee, Mount Pleasant Golf Club, White Mountains near Bretton Woods, New Hampshire", circa 1890 - 1905.

4. "Golferinos", circa 1905.

5. Holing out at number one, circa 1920.

6. "Justices of the Supreme Court at play", circa 1925.

5

4

6

up easily with a cheerful smile, and, although his reputation as a talker is not great, he replies readily and to the point to all questions. Indeed, he submitted most gracefully to the volley of questions literally fired at him during the two days after his arrival.

Alexander H. Findlay, the head professional in Florida, and who has charge of many courses around Boston, has a deep admiration for the personal and golfing qualities of Vardon, whom he had the pleasure of playing in a friendly match of fifty-four holes last Fall in England. Findlay has written the following excellent account of Vardon, which, coming from a brother golfer, can hardly be improved upon:

"Let me in a few words give you an idea of what Harry is like. In the first place, he differs from me very much, as he is quite nice looking, and is greatly admired by the ladies. I weigh 155 pounds; so does Vardon to an ounce. I stand 5 feet 11 inches; so does Vardon exactly. I drive a fairly good ball; he drives a better, (I don't mean quality, I mean distance.) Vardon is exceptionally quiet and unassuming, free from the wickedness and vices that often beset young golf professionals. He smokes a briar pipe all the while during a friendly match, is seldom on the aggressive regarding conversation, etc., speaks when he is spoken to, and that very politely. He is passionately fond of golf and association football. The latter is the great Winter pastime there, and Vardon will go a long distance to witness a game, providing it doesn't clash with his golf appointments."

A good deal has been said about Vardon's style in playing. It is true that he is not a representative of the orthodox system of golf. His style of play will not be found in any of the numerous books on "How to Play Golf." Vardon does not go by rules, but by what comes naturally and easily to him, and his rules are those of experience and observation from long practice on the links. J.H. Taylor, the former English champion, has a great deal of Vardon's style.

"I know that neither Taylor nor myself go by the books," said Vardon last week, "yet between us we have won five out of the last six open championships. We were the pioneers in gripping the club with overlapping fingers; and also the first to use short shafts for the wooden head clubs. The short clubs have now been very generally adopted by amateurs and professionals throughout England. The shorter handles give me a better command of the club, for there are no protruding ends to get in the way.

Vardon brought over thirteen clubs with him. "They are all beauties, too," he said, "the pick of nearly four hundred that I have used at different times."

This set consists of two drivers, one brassey, two driving mashies, two cleeks, two putters, a niblick, two lofters, and a special club of his own make, having a deep face resembling the driving mashie. One of the putters is known as a goose-neck putter, from the shape of the iron above the head. That putter Vardon would not part with for many times its original cost, for he has had it three years, and used it in two of his open championship victories. He generally uses a cleek for a long putt and the for goose-neck for putting on the green. Unlike many foreign players, Vardon does not use a wooden putter.

Vardon will remain in the United States until about the middle of May, when he will return to England to defend his title to the open championship in the annual tournament which will be played in June on the old St. Andrews Links, Scotland.

– New York Times, 1900

GOLF BOOMED BY TAFT

The fact that President Taft has chosen golf as the best out-of-door sport to keep him in good physical condition is responsible for an unprecedented congestion of players on the city's golf courses, according to the men who have charge of the various links.

The number of players, it is said, on the Van Cortlandt and the Forest Park links have more than doubled since Taft's election and the publicity which has attended the President's almost daily play. In a way, it is pointed out, the fact is indicative that Americans are imitative in their patriotism, and diligently follow the examples set by the head of the Nation.

Within the last few weeks many new lockers have been added to the clubhouse at Van Cortlandt, and there is a waiting list of applicants for more than double the number of lockers now in use. At the Forest Park Clubhouse the congestion is even worse.

"The fact that golf is President Taft's favorite game is undoubtedly responsible for the great increase in the number of players this year." said Tom White, the keeper of the Van Cortlandt Clubhouse. "Last year it used to be tennis, because that was President Roosevelt's hobby. Now the tennis courts are almost deserted, except for the habitual players.

"Many of this year's golf players are of an entirely

---

7. "Number one tee, Hampton Terrace Golf Course, Augusta, Georgia", circa 1905.

8. "White Mountain House Club", circa 1895 - 1910. Note the accompanying dogs and portable caddie.

Following spread, 9. "Clock golf at the Royal Palm, Miami, Florida." The boy at the center right drags the sand green.

7

8

29

9

10

11

different calibre from those of former years and they show in many ways that the President's partialiy for the game has influenced them largely in taking up the sport. These admirers are easily singled out. They constantly discuss the fine points of the President's game as they read about it in the papers and have long discussions as to the kinds of clubs the President uses.

"This idea is now so widespread that an enterprising firm has put out the 'Taft putter' of which numbers are being used. It is just an indication of the way people allow those in high places to set the fashion for them in other things besides dress.

"I expect the craze to increase from now on until the end of the President's term, and, certainly, if it keeps up at the present rate, the city will have to establish new golf links to take care of the players. Even now it is almost impossible to play on the public courses on Saturdays, Sundays, and holidays, the congestion is so great."

Reports of greatly increased attendance at private golf clubs all over the country show that the interest in the game is not confined to any one locality, but has spread generally.

–New York Times, 1909

THE WOMAN'S GAME

The organization of the Women's Metropolitan Golf League would seem to indicate the approach of some solid foundation for the game in our country as a woman's sport, and this first attempt at organization brings into prominence one or two problems, upon the proper solution of which much depends. What are the possibilities and what are the limitations of the game for women as a whole? The variance of the scores of even our best players from year to year suggests to many the thought that we have no stability whatever, and the further fact that so few women, among the large number who play, have succeeded in scoring under a hundred, raises the doubt as to whether the actual scientific game is within our reach at all. Among men, golf is constantly progressing; new stars overthrowing old favorites has become a part of the history of every great tournament. Can women say the same of their game and of themselves, and how do they stand in comparison with men?

10. By the early 1900's the golf course was fast becoming a businessman's ideal alternative to a stuffy meeting room.

11. Refinements in the swing were rapidly taking place by 1915 as this golfer at Brown's Well Golf Course, Hazelhurst, Mississippi impressively demonstrates.

12. "Charlevioux, Michigan Golf Links", circa 1900, at the 660 yard first tee.

Following spread, 13. Putting on the eighth green, Stevens House Golf Links, Lake Placid, New York, circa 1909.

12

13

14

15

It is a "sign of the times," a significant indication of the steady march of progress, that men and women are constantly drawing comparisons between each other. We have grown accustomed to this, and it is only when we approach a comparison in the subject of athletics in any form that we realize that the emancipation of women has been almost entirely intellectual, not physical. Forced forward by necessity, conviction, or ambition, we have thrown our brain power into competition with men, and have gained for ourselves an honorable place among artists, workers, and breadwinners. But physically where are we? A thousand times better off than we used to be, but far, how very far, from what we some day hope to be.

That we should be physically inferior is only the logical effect of an easily discovered cause. Born with less strength to begin with, we have had no systematic training in physical development, and what nature tried to do for us herself, fashion and conventionality speedily destroyed. While our brothers were playing baseball or climbing cherry trees, we were sitting with our feet dangling from a high piano stool, thrumming finger exercises, melancholy and submission stamped on the droop of our two little pig-tails. When the boys went to college and tried for the 'Varsity', we in our turn went to school and developed along with them our brains, our accomplishments, and our perceptions of people and things, but there we stopped. Lately the bicycle has done more to emancipate us from the tyranny of clothes and conventionality than anything that has ever been given us. Oh! Those first days,when in short skirt, easy shirtwaist, and a hat that would actually stay on, we flew along the winding , blossoming country roads free as the air we breathed. There has been no sensation since quite like it, yet we seem to be unfaithful to our first love. It is because still another sport has been given us, which needs less violent exertion than bicycling, yet requires nerve, skill, strength, endurance, and self-mastery. People say bicycling has gone out,. riding has gone out, that golf will go out. This is not true. Each sport will find its proper space and sphere of usefulness. The first two

16

Before the invention of the golf tee in 1920, golfers used a pinch of sand to tee the ball. Most "teeing grounds" were constructed of sand and a box of sand was usually stored nearby. 14. A pastoral view from the elevated tee at Green Park Golf Course, Green Park , North Carolina.

15. "Golf at St. Augustine, Florida".

16. Marion Hollins, 1921 U.S. Ladies Champion, demonstrates an enviable follow-through and a fierce competitiveness not anticipated from the fairer sex.

17. Once slaves to fashion that restricted free movement, the ladies originally made poor competitors.

Following spread 18. A young lady goes through her practice swings at the well manicured and maintained first tee in Palm Beach, Florida, circa 1904.

17

have only ceased to be a fashionable fad. Golf is rapidly losing that character. We can now look about us and see exactly where we stand.

Bicycling is not and cannot be a game. Golf is distinctly a contest. When women took up golf, they not only had to learn to play that game, but a game. Tennis among women seemed to have been confined to comparatively few. Men have played games all their lives – they and their fathers before them. They have competed all their lives, and will go on competing to the end. Life is the same old question of the "survival of the fittest." Primitive man fought for his daily bread with a pointed stick or a jagged stone. Modern man sits in his office and fights with his brains. It is the same object, only the method of attaining it has changed. In consequence, in golf, as in every contest, men have the advantage over women of familiarity with competitive play. That it is hard for us to get accustomed to competition is proved by the results of the first matches three or four years ago. Our practice scores were good for beginners, but our competitive medal scores were simply heartbreaking. It is largely so still; the nervous element and the strain of competing against the whole field accounts for the difference of many a point between practice and competitive play. In match play there is the keenest kind of competition, but it is narrowed down to one individual, who is before your eyes, who plays along with you stroke for stroke, who stumbles and falls, and recovers just as you do, taking your mind completely off that worst of all hob-goblins, a good score. Woman's greatest difficulty seems to be in the long game. Some people consider it almost insurmountable. To my mind, however, it can be overcome. In low scoring, aside from a general accuracy, careful study leads to the conclusion that the second shot is the most important. A long drive by a man or a woman is a poor affair if the second shot is foozled, yet a poor drive has sometimes been retrieved by a brilliant brassey. Herein lies our first best chance, as a brassey for some unknown reason is a woman's best club. Realizing this, she uses and abuses it, often taking it for a comparatively short approach, because the lie is tempting, or more especially because she is absolutely at sea and helpless regarding distances varying from thirty-five yards to seventy-five. What she gains by a good drive and a good brassey she throws away by her wretched long approach. It has become something of a cant phrase to say that women approach and putt well. They do putt beautifully and approach well, twenty yards away from the green, but about the real approach, which is usually the third shot, varying form thirty-five yards to seventy-five, women as yet know nothing. This means that we are weak on our long irons, and every woman who really wishes to round out her game and lower her score permanently should concentrate her attention on first her second shot, and second, her cleek and her mid-iron. The two latter she should practice every day of her life. She is sure to work at her drive and brassey, the reward is so great, but the long irons are uninteresting in comparison, and in consequence, women have failed to recognize their importance.

In the matter of regular practice we are also somewhat hampered. A man after he has been a few years out of college generally settles down to two things, his business and his exercise, which is usually his pleasure. He makes an appointment to play golf, and he keeps it with the same precision that he keeps a business appointment. If he does not, the other man is usually anxious to know the reason why. A woman, whether married or single, never gives up her social life, and although it is a general impression among some men that she has really nothing to do, her hours, and minutes even, are filled with a thousand and one things – business and pleasure running into each other at all seasons and all hours. She makes an engagement to play golf, and a dozen household or charitable, or social, or educational duties pull the other way, and in despair golf goes to the wall. In Midsummer a woman has more time for regular practice, and it is for this reason that in May her scores are high, and in October low, after the freedom and healthful open air life and opportunities for hard work. This leads us to the belief that practice and intelligent study will bring a really scientific game within the reach of any woman who has actual golfing ability. The rising generation should produce some fine players, equal to Beatrix Hoyt or Lady Margaret Scott. Both of these women had the exceptional advantages of beginning when very young. Beatrix Hoyt was only fifteen when she won her first championship at Morristown, and Lady Margaret Scott handled the clubs as a child and learned the game playing with her father and brothers. There is a certain ease which comes from beginning early, which is not usually attainable when the game is taken up later. Lady Margaret Scott has a very long and powerful swing, acquired of course from playing constantly with men. She did what she saw others do. A woman can do nothing that will improve her game as much in practice as to play a man's course with some of her friends. The fact that she must work, must carry the obstacles, gives her just the stimulus she needs. Nothing is so great a help to progress as to be obliged to do something that you yourself think,

19. *"Pitch & putt golf, Lahyoya Lodge, Napa Valley, California"*

Excellent 9-hole course laid out by John Duncan Dunn.

An ideal summer resort for New York business men. Within an hour's run from East 34th Street, New York City, or Flatbush Avenue, Brooklyn.

SURF AND STILL WATER BATHING. BOATING, SAILING, AND FISHING

NEVER UNCOMFORTABLY WARM. TEN DEGREES COOLER THAN ANY OTHER RESORT ON THE ATLANTIC COAST

A. E. DICK, Proprietor, New York Office, 12 West 23d Street, N. Y.

19a

19b

Aided by golf schools, inspired by professional exhibitions and elegantly accommodated at plush resorts, the number of American golfers mushroomed in the early 1900's. The primary facilitators of the boom, however, were the railway and the automobile which transported a nation to the courses.

Following spread 20. "Public links, East Potomac Park, Washington, D.C.", circa 1923.

19c

19e

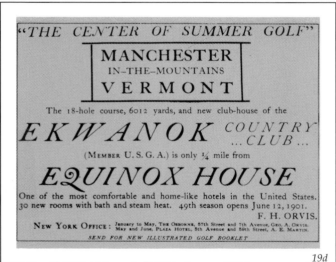

of golf as a man, simply because nature, for her own inscrutable ends, designed us the weaker vessel, but a woman can make her golf a truly great boon; she can bring to it every bit of mind and nerve and skill and endurance and sportsmanship that she has in her whole body; she can learn to win without vain boasting, and lose with a good grace, and in so doing take upon herself the complexion of those who play the game, not for silver cups or newspaper notoriety, but for the actual enduring love of it.

– Lilian Brooke, writing in the New York Times, 1900

3,500,000 GOLF PLAYERS

The total number of men and women who play golf is greater than the total number of men and women who watch and play baseball, according to The Cleveland Plain Dealer. Golf is becoming a national game, because both men and women can play the game. Baseball has its devotees only in the masculine ranks. Women can watch the game, but few can either understand or play it.

Baseball is too strenuous for the person who does not play regularly. Many play until they reach 21. After that they quit the game as a regular form of exercise and pleasure, unless they go into the professional ranks. But golf is a game for all ages. The old as well as the young can play. It gives one as much fresh air as does baseball,

but particularly someone else thinks, is just a little beyond you, and for this reason the idea of women withdrawing altogether and having clubs or courses of their own is not a good one. It is true that at Morristown and Philadelphia, where such clubs first flourished, women have attained the highest golfing standard so far. Women do not run these clubs entirely by themselves.

A little patience, much courage, belief in ourselves, and the same generous help and encouragement from men, and women's golf as a true sport will be on a firm foundation. The best result as a whole that she can hope to attain is, after all, to play as good a comparative game

20a

21

"The Swing", that singular, poetic, fluid movement; that cerebral, muscular and anatomical harmony, has been pursued, studied, and discussed for over one hundred years now, and we still haven't gotten it right. This quest is, for even the most serious golfer, a descent to the ridiculous as demonstrated by Charles Mack to renowned champ, Walter Hagen. Grip and stance are a bit untraditional, but note the straight left arm.

Following spread 24. "Second green on Eagles Move, Pennsylvania," 1920.

23

he great adopted game, Golf, "teeing off,"
Copyright, 1909, by Stereo-Travel Co.

ALEX FINLEY, SCARSDALE GOLF CLUB   456-11

22

and keeps one healthy without straining the muscles.

Those who could afford to play baseball can afford to play golf. It is not much more expensive. A set of golfing clubs, balls and other equipment does not cost much more than a baseball uniform, a half dozen bats, spiked shoes and other baseball paraphernalia.

There are in America today something like 600 golfing clubs allied with the United States Golf Association. That represents a golf population of at least 500,000. That is only a small part of the army of golfers. In every city where there are public links there are many golfers not associated with golfing clubs. They play either on the public links or on the private links at the invitation of some friend who happens to be a member of a club.

There are between 2,500,000 and 3,500,000 golfers in America today. When the big cities have completed their proposed public links the golfing army will be perhaps increased 2,000,000. It is estimated that there are about 200,000 golfers in New York City and vicinity, while there are about 800,000 in the State. Pennsylvania has about 400,000 putters.

Even for the spectator, golf has more beneficial results. At a baseball game the spectator watches the play from the grandstand. At a golf match the spectators must do as much "leg work" as the players. He has to walk over the entire course if he wants to see all the play. Thus the golf spectators get almost as much beneficial exercise as the golfer, while the only thing a baseball fan gets is cramped limbs and fresh air. In chilly weather the golf spectator can walk around and keep warm. The fan must sit in the stand and suffer chills.

"What is there about this game of golf that has increased its player from the 5,000 of ten years ago to the 2,500,000 or 3,500,000 of today?" is the question. And the answer is: "Try the game once."

–New York Times, 1915

VAST IMPROVEMENT IN WOMEN GOLFERS

When Howard F. Whitney, Secretary of the U.S.G.A., announced recently that the women golfers would be allowed to select their own course and dates for the 1917 championship, it was not taken as an indication of the "feministic" trend of modern times, nor even as a tribute to the superwoman, who, now that she has become acclimated, will doubtless appear on the links next season, but it was the fitting official recognition that the 1916 season saw greater improvement in women's golf than in any other department of the game in this country.

It has long been the wail of many golf experts that America had few women golfers, or perhaps none at all, who could safely and sanely be placed in the same category with the fair golfers of Great Britain and Ireland. When Miss Muriel Dodd and the former Miss Gladys Ravenscroft appeared at the women's national championship at Wilmington in 1913, they seemed so much superior to the native American golfers that pessimistic prophets agreed unanimously on the dismal

D is the Duffer, the Drive
    that he cuts,
And the Something he says when he
    misses short putts.

24a

M is the Moment of
    agony keen
When it's one for the Match
    on the very last green.

24b

N is the Niblick, retriever
    of blunders,
And now and again it accomplishes
    wonders.

24e

O is the Odd that we play
    for the tin, —
Peculiar indeed that it
    doesn't get in.

24f

outlook in women's golf for a decade to come.

The play of the youthful women's national champion of 1916, Miss Alexa Stirling of Atlanta is alone enough evidence to overturn these prophecies, but the outlook becomes even brighter after a scrutiny of the season's records of some of the other women golfers in the season which has just drawn to a close. Not to speak of the acquisition of Mrs. W.A. Gavin, who played from an American club in the national championship tournament this year, this tournament was marked by the fine play of four American women golfers, Miss Stirling, the ultimate winner; Miss Mildred Caverly, runner-up, and the two semifinalists, Mrs. Thomas Hucknall and Mrs. C.C. Auchincloss, both metropolitan golfers. In addition to

the individual play of these women, the successful team competition that the Women's Metropolitan Golf Association carried through its busiest season has given an impetus to women's golf that will carry it far in the coming year.

Of the work of Miss Stirling through the season nothing need be said except that she won everything in sight. Starting with the Southern championship at Chattanooga, where she won medal, title, driving, approaching, and putting contests, she continued her victorious march through the Huntingdon Valley tournament for the Berthellyn trophy, defeating then national champion, Mrs. C.H. Vanderbeck of the Philadelphia Cricket Club by a decisive margin, and she

R is the Rub that may lay us up dead, Or leave us in sand buried over the head.

24c

G is the Game we expected to play, But which didn't come off on the tournament day.

24d

X is the X-pletive sometimes employed, For a golfer is human, and easily annoyed.

24g

Z is for Zero, the sign of despair, ''Awa' wi' your gowf! we will play it nae moir.''

24h

fittingly closed the season by winning the national championship at Belmont Spring in early October.

It is not so much what she won, but the manner in which she did it that brings so much glory to this nineteen-year-old Southern girl, and so much pride to the women's golfing contingent in general. After watching her through tournament after tournament, John G. Anderson and other capable critics have pronounced her not a "fine woman golfer," but just a "fine golfer," with all that goes to make up a first-class individual of this rare species. Taught from her early childhood by the keen eye and the astute brain of Steward Maiden, the Atlanta professional, Miss Stirling plays every shot in the very mode and method of her

24 - 24h. Famed sporting artist, A.B. Frost, illustrated this golfers alphabet, true to golf and golfer today as it was in the late 1800's.

25, 26 and 27. Cartoon styles have changed, but not the spirit and character of the golfer.

Following spread 25. "In trouble at seventh hole, Mount Pleasant Golf Links", circa 1900 - 1905. Note the golfer in middleground hacking out of the bunker, and palatial building in distance.

instructor. Only one other amateur golfer plays with the entrancing style of the women's national champion and that is Bobbie Jones, Georgia State amateur champion, another pupil of Steward Maiden, who considerably enlivened things for Bob Gardner and other prominent golfers in the national amateur championship at Merion.

The runner-up to Miss Stirling in the national championship at Belmont Spring, Miss Mildred Caverly of the Philadelphia Cricket Club, is another of the younger set who has come forward rapidly in the last season. She is now the possessor of the Philadelphia title, and in her quest for the Berthellyn trophy and the national championship, it required the full powers of Miss Stirling to turn her from her goal.

A fine free player, especially from the tee, the young Philadelphian has a brilliant future in golf before her if she continues her progress. At Belmont Spring she profited by the help of two very capable instructors who were aiding her to perfect that ever-inefficient department known as the short game. One was Stewart Maiden, the Atlanta professional; the other was Miss Alexa Stirling, her conqueror in the final match for the title. On the afternoon before the final contest the ultimate winner spent the better part of an hour instructing her prospective opponent in the mysteries of the chip shot.

The play of Miss Stirling and Miss Caverly was no surprise, however, but what did cause astonishment was the appearance of two metropolitan players, Mrs. C.C. Auchincloss of Piping Rock and Mrs. Thomas Hucknall

That January Feeling —

Copyright, 1921, by Herbert Johnson.

Herbert Johnson

IN TROUBLE AT SEVENTH HOLE
MOUNT PLEASANT GOLF LINKS

26

27

Stereoscopic sequence, circa 1900 - 1905, pokes fun at love on the links;

26. Aroused by the cries of the fair maid and lover, The players laughed til they could scarcely recover.

27. On vengeance bent, the wraithful lover started, While Fannie hid her face quite broken-hearted.

Following spread 28. Teeing off into a stiff wind at Stevens House Golf Links, Lake Placid, New York, circa 1909.

071224, STEVENS HOUSE GOLF LINKS, LAKE PLACID, ADIRONDACK MTS., N.Y.

29, 30 and 31. Despite close grooming by "state-of-the-art" equipment, yesterdays greens were rougher than todays fairways.

Following spread 32. A rough-and-ready crew of Baltusrol, New Jersey caddies.

29

30

of Forest Hill, in the semi-final round. Certainly metropolitan golfers had a right to high position, but these were not the particular New York representatives that were looked upon for such brilliant performances. Mrs. Hucknall had taken up the game at a comparatively recent date, and Mrs. Auchincloss was playing in her first national tournament.

Mrs. Hucknall expected nothing but summary elimination when she faced the former national and international champion, Mrs J.V. Hurd of Pittsburgh, in the first round. She won this match, however, and then defeated Miss Ethel Campbell of Philadelphia and Miss Laurie Kaiser, runner-up in the Western championship, before she succumbed to Miss Caverly in the semi-final round. Mrs. Auchincloss had two sensational battles on the Belmont links. To the utter astonishment of herself and the assembled multitude, she defeated Mrs. William A. Gavin, women's Eastern champion, and one of the favorites for the title, in the third round of match play. As if this were not enough distinction for a tournament tyro, she played against Miss Stirling on the following day and was the only player in the tournament who carried the women's national champion to the home green, where the last putt by the Atlanta girl decided the match.

With the sterling work of these golfers in the national championship, and with such players as Mrs. Vanderbeck and Mrs. Q.F. Feltner, five times the metropolitan champion, held in reserve for the coming season, the outlook for women's golf in America is more than hopeful – it is bright.
– New York Times, 1916

GOLF CONTINUES TO BOOM IN THE COLONIES

Although golf in America is still in its swaddling clothes as compared with the game on the other side of the Atlantic, it has much to be proud of, for unquestionably the royal sport has worked wonders in a comparatively short time. It is doubtful if even the most optimistic devotee of driver and iron ten years ago would have dared to predict that in 1910 golf would give employment to thousands, and add to the attractions of hundreds of towns and villages. Had he ventured such a prediction he probably would have been placed in the same category as the man who prophesied that a heavier-than-air machine could fly from New York to Philadelphia.

Time has shown that golf is not a pastime to be taken lightly, but, rather, seriously. Practically every other game has its limitations as to season. Not so with golf, for only a foot or more of snow will prevent the golfer from making his rounds of the links, and weather is never too hot to prevent it, either.

33

34

36

CAMERON B. BUXTON

35

No longer does the man in the street gaze at the golfer with his set of clubs as a curiosity. Nor is the "hockey player" remark so frequently heard. One might hear a man of the navy type inform his friend that golf is a "rotten game," but even this is a sign of progress, for he knows it is golf and not hockey.

The huge strides golf is making, and has made, is conclusive proof of its fascination. Ten years ago the golfer had to travel much longer to reach a golf course that he does at present. Every town of any size at all has its golf course. No seaside resort is a complete success unless it has its own links, and it is the knowledge that golf is to be had that frequently brings the visitor and his family. This is also true of many inland resorts.

This means business for the resort or the village in or near which the course is located. Even in ten years Garden City has made big strides in the way of improvement and much of it is due to the golf course there. Incidentally, Garden City now has two courses, the second being the Salisbury links, over which the recent tournament of the Eastern Professional Golfers' Association was played.

This is by no means an exceptional case, for there are a great many other cities and towns where similar instances might be cited. Landowners are quick to realize the fact that the ground they have hitherto looked upon as being scarcely worthy of consideration is

"In the history of American field sports," wrote the New York Times in 1895, "there can be found no outdoor pastime that developed and attained such popularity in such a short period of time as the game of golf." No less remarkable is how the game has retained that popularity through world wars, a depression, changing fashion and a series of generations.

Following spread 37. For every 2,000 courses, 18 holes; for every 18 holes, a clubhouse. Bass Rocks Golf Clubhouse, Glouster, Massachusetts, circa 1900.

O 72108 BASS ROCKS GOLF CLUB HOUSE, GLOUCESTER, MASS.

66

38

38 and 39. In barely over two decades, golf evolved from the eccentric diversions of several Yonkers businessmen to the coveted pleasure of the upper crust and, finally, the passionate pastime of an entire nation. Its challenges and special, sweet rewards were open to everyone, regardless of status, ability, or disability.

Following spread ?????????

valuable, from a golfing point of view, and he charges more per acre for it than he does for his best agricultural land.

With regard to the employment that the game provides it is difficult to estimate it. Professionals and their assistants, ground-keepers, caretakers, iron headmakers, golf ball makers, etc., are dependent upon the game, while there are thousands of boys, and even men, who make their living as caddies. The list could be considerably increased, even to those who earn their livelihood by making mixtures for the extermination of worms and other ground pests.

It seems a pity that the expenses of golf are such as to debar those who have scarcely more than a comfortable income from participating in the pleasures of the game, but even this may soon be relieved, for at present there are public links which are very well patronized by persons in ordinary walks of life. It is quite possible, however, that in a few years various municipalities will take more of an interest in the sport than at present, for, rapid as the growth of the game has been, it still is in its infancy.

From the health point of view golf is a well-known preserver of youth, not only being prescribed by physicians as a health restorer, but being played by physicians themselves who practice what they preach.

– New York Times, 1910

40

FASHION

Copyright 1906
Celebrity Art

2. *"Kitty's at the First Tee", from a drawing by W.T. Smedley appearing in Harper's Weekly, 1897.*

FASHION

PASSING OF THE HOBO GOLFER

The day when the golfer thought it was necessary to look like a tramp to play good golf is passed, according to The Washington Post. Golf clothing is now as formal as the dress suit. At one time, any sort of "duds" was worn, and it was a common thing to see the most heterogeneous collection of clothing on the course. This never applied to women players, for they have always presented a neat appearance, for no woman likes to look unattractive, particularly to other women.

It was not an unusual sight to see a big car drive up to the clubhouse and unload alot of men golfers whose dress was the last thing in the sartorial line. Ten minutes later the same crowd would make their appearance at the first tee in the worst lot of clothing imaginable.

Most of the golfers would wear the oldest sort of sweaters, soiled shirts, without collar or tie, and trousers smeared with dirt they had rubbed from their hands after teeing. Some would wear coats and some were without the one thing that is absolutely necessary to the English golfer. It was never possible to tell the station of the golfer from his golfing costumes. Even men who wear evening clothes nearly every evening in the week were not guiltless.

Then all of a sudden things changed. Golfers came to realize that it was possible to be comfortable in well-fitting clothes; that it was possible to wear both collar and tie without interfering with the golf; that soiled shirts and trousers were no longer derigueur. Tailors began to make a specialty of golf clothing and the knickerbockers of our youth began to make their appearance on the links in great number. As a result, the sloppily clad player is the exception now. Men as well as women are as well dressed on the links as off.

It took some golfers years to realize that it is possible to play golf in a coat. Men would wear sweaters, for these gave them plenty of freedom, but any tailor can build a coat that has the same advantages as the sweater. Naturally, as the weather becomes warmer, the coat is laid aside.

Over in Great Britain, not to wear a coat on the links is as bad as driving a ball off a putting green. It is a custom that has been handed down for a century or more. In tennis and in other sports over there it is not necessary to don the coat, but it is just as essential a part of the golfer's clothing as are shoes. And this custom is the one that proved so much of a handicap for the American players.

With the exception of Walter J. Travis – who is an

1. *"Golf girl", 1906.*

4

3

3 & 4. At the turn of the century, women golfers leaned more toward fashion than function. Gargantuan hats and restrictive clothing scored big with the gents, but lead also to big scores on the links.

5. By 1920 styles conformed themselves toward better golf while staying above par from the men's perspective.

Following spread 6. Ladies on the practice green at Hotel Champlain, Blue Point, New York, circa 1900.

8

T.H. POLHEMUS OF N.Y. 322-

9

7, 8, 9, & 10. The booming interest in American golf created an entire new range of opportunities for designers, clothiers and

11. Undergarment manufacturers.

Following spread 12. A splendid shot of the crowd, typifying the fashions of 1900, watching the great J.H. Taylor driving off the first tee at Mount Pleasant House, White Mountains.

7

10

12

Australian – none of the big American players wears a coat in mid-summer. Being forced to wear them in the British amateur championship was quite a hardship.

British professionals who play here soon get used to American habits, and you will find them playing well without coats.

–New York Times, 1914

BAL POUDRE?

The August season, which is the gayest at this all-the-year-round resort, was most auspiciously ushered in tonight with numerous informal suppers.

Invitations are being issued for the usual private affairs that are the big features of the Summer season here. They will include a bal poudre, two subscriptions and numerous private Germans and cotillions, the dansants, supper dansants, and a garden fete.

The season never is really dedicated until the dancing of the "White Sulphur Riley," a stately minuet, which for seventy-odd years has been danced at least once each season. It is danced by women only, and this week it preceded a ball, followed by a supper dansant. Those dancing it included Miss Hilah C. French of New York, Mrs. Sydney Wynne Ffoulkes, Mrs. J. Kellogg Bradley, the Misses Bertha and Frances Clark of Philadelphia, Miss Doris Haywood of Washington, Mrs. John D. Potts, and Miss Nell Potts of Richmond.

– Report of the White Sulphur Springs Country Club, 1914

LIBBERS

With all our new independence and liberty and power, men still watch over us with the old chivalry, plan for us, and push us forward to still greater freedom. The country clubs are now looking after our golf and are doing more to further our interests than we could hope to do by ourselves. Of course, there is some dear old gentleman, to whom the sight of a petticoat on the golf links is like a red rag to a bull, but he is generally forgiven, as we know his wife has spoiled him, and his daughter neglected his education. When a young man is bothered by a fluttering skirt in the distance it is usually because he has no other serious occupation.

– New York Times, 1910

14

13

15

13. *For a short time, men lead the fashion parade by adopting the traditional short red tunics of their St. Andrews, Scotland brethren. This affectation did not last long, however, as the jackets proved restrictive and too warm. Men's fashion sunk into a temporary doldrum as...*

14, 15, *and* 16. *women's fashion explored new horizons.*

16

17

18

A sampling of men's fashion styles through an approximate 30-year period:

17. Stiff, starched collars of a dapper group at White Mountain, New Hampshire, circa 1895.

18. A golf outing of the Knights Templar Society along the Mississippi Golf Coast, circa 1925.

19. J.H. Taylor, circa 1900 - 1905, one of several renowned British golfers who toured the U.S. helped create interest in golf as well as notions about golfing fashion.

20

21

20, 21, and 22. Walter "the Hag" Hagen was not merely an early American golf hero, but its first true personality. While most golf pros of the era were considered crusty and literally unworthy of using the front door of the clubhouse, the dapper, charismatic Hagen became friends with no less than Prince Edwards of Wales (with Hagen at right as "the Hag" accepts his 1928 British Open trophy). "I don't want to be a millionaire," he once quipped, "I just want to live like one". And certainly he did, while along the way making a heavy influence on American golfing fashion - including the demonstrative statement that pullover sweaters not only look spiffy on the links, they were less restrictive than the tweedy coats of the day.

23. *Touring British professional, Edward Ray, and…*

24. *U.S. pro, Tom McNamara fashion were emulated by casual golfers who hoped better scores would also follow.*

23

24

447. EDWARD RAY —

1100. THOMAS McNAMARA —

25

25 and 26.

26

REFINEMENTS

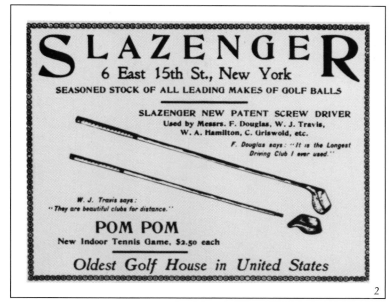

2. *Stazenger not only manufactured screw-on drivers, but inventoried a "seasoned stock" of golf balls.*

REFINEMENTS

TRAVIS EXPLAINS NEW GOLFING CODE

In golfing circles it is but natural that the new code of rules which will go into effect with the new year has attracted widespread attention, for while there are no radical changes, a number of important amendments have been made to the old formula with which it will be absolutely necessary for golfers to be familiar. Some criticisms have been made to certain of the changes abroad, but the general consensus of opinion is that what changes have been authorized will make for the better conduct and appreciation of the game. The United States Golf Association, which sent a carefully prepared draft of recommendations last Spring to the Rules Committee of the Royal and Ancient Club of St. Andrews, Scotland, will formally adopt the new code at its annual meeting early in January, and there is not the slightest indication that a single objection will be made to any portion of the accepted code.

Walter J. Travis, who has made as close a study of the technicalities of golf as any one in this country, has issued an unqualified indorsement of the new code, and as editor of The American Golfer he says, in the current number:

"The new rules, as a whole, will be hailed with delight and universal approval by all loyal supporters and true lovers of the royal and ancient game, and their thanks will go forth not only to the Rules of Golf Committee of St. Andrews, but also to the present officials of the United States Golf Association, which organization for the first time in its history has been officially recognized and represented in the councils of the governing body. No one, in going carefully over the new rules, can fail to be profoundly impressed with the prodigious amount of thoughtful care bestowed on their compilation."

In dealing with some of the changes in detail, Mr. Travis says that they must be frankly admitted as distinctly in the line of improvements over the former code. Railways and fences will no longer be regarded as hazards, but permanent grass within a hazard is to be considered part of the hazard. This omission in the old rules, says Mr. Travis, read in conjunction with the new rule simply means that at present when a ball is in a hazard, whether it be on grass or not, the club shall not be so led under penalty of the loss of the hole, implying that now all hazards must be carefully defined.

Mr. Travis approves heartily of the change which prevents a golfer from using the back of his hand to smooth

---

1. *Not even the remotest sector of golf was safe from the inventor's guile: "Mouse Trap Armor for Golf Caddies - Here is the newest safety device for golf courses. It is designed somewhat like a giant mousetrap and protects caddies and ball-retrievers from wild golf balls."*

5. Some companies ignored the war of the ball manufacturers and made a living selling "retreads".

4. British pro Harry Vardon made his 20,000 mile American tour to promote a new, gutta-percha ball carrying his name, the "Vardon Flyer". Understandable then, his unwillingness to switch to the Haskell.

3. The Haskell Ball, invented by American, Coburn Haskell, appeared at the turn of the century. Wound with rubber filaments under tension, then covered with gutta percha (a rubbery substance), the Haskell outflew the solid gutta-percha in many tests and contests. It was not until the U.S. Open of 1901, however, that it began to replace the old guttas. Walter Travis, one of only 20 players in the field of 124 using the Haskell, won the event. Many stubborn pros refused to give up the traditional gutta perchas, Harry Vardon among them. Harry's decline in tournament play is said to have been attributed to the new technology.

down the line of his putt. Commenting on this, he says:

"Loose impediments may be lifted from the putting green and dung. Worm casts, snow, and ice may be lightly scraped aside with a club, but otherwise the line of putt must not be touched. Brushing with the hand means the loss of the hole. A very important change, and a most excellent one".

"It is gratifying to note," adds Mr. Travis, "the reinstatement of the rules of etiquette in the regular code and also the addition of several desirable features, including the duties of players looking for a lost ball. In this connection it will be observed that the section has been amplified which stipulates that players looking for a lost ball should allow other matches coming up to pass them; they should signal to the players following them to pass, and having given such signal they should not continue their play until these players have passed and are out of reach."

Other important alterations are: No one shall stand to mark the line of play through the green or from a hazard. Penalty, loss of the hole.

It is no longer necessary to drop a ball from the head. Face the hole, stand erect, and drop behind, over the shoulder.

Under no circumstances shall a practice swing be taken anywhere, except on the tee, when the ball is not in play, under penalty of loss of the hole.

Casual water on a putting green is now practically nonexistent. When a ball is on a green a clear putt to the hole is permissible, free from intervening water.

On the much-mooted question as to whether stymies shall be played or not, Mr. Travis says:

"Stymies form an integral part of the code, and, therefore, should be played. They are defensible on the ground that they are capable of being negotiated by the exercise of the highest degree of skill. In match play competition, it is absolutely essential that all contestants should be compelled to play stymies, otherwise great injustice may be worked. The new rules make their playing compulsory under penalty of disqualification."

– New York Times, 1908

"GUTTY" LOSES IN TEST.

London, April 2. – Great interest was attached to a golf match over the Sandy Lodge course today, in consequence of a heated discussion of the respective merits of the old solid india-rubber ball known as the "gutty" and the modern rubber-cored ball, first introduced from America. Taylor and Braid opposed Vardon and Duncan in a four-ball match over thirty-six holes.

One couple played with "gutties" and the other couple with "rubber cores" for the first eighteen holes, each side changing balls for the second eighteen holes. The result, as was expected, ended in a victory for the "rubber cores."

Vardon and Duncan, using the modern ball, were 5 up on their opponents at the end of the first round. Changing to "gutties" in the afternoon, Vardon and Duncan lost four of these five holes, gaining the victory on two rounds by 1 up. The net victory for the "rubber cores" thus was nine holes in thirty-six.

During the afternoon a driving competition was held. Braid driving a rubber-cored ball 278 yards and Duncan sending a "gutty" 240. The test clearly showed the advantage of the rubber-cored ball, certainly in distance of "run" after the ball's first bounce, and proved conclusively that it made golf easier for the ordinary player, although the difference it made to champions was not so great as might be expected. The best round with the "gutty" was Braid's 70, and the best round with a rubber core was Vardon's 67.

– New York Times, 1914

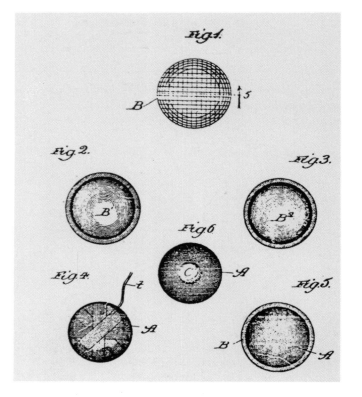

7

8

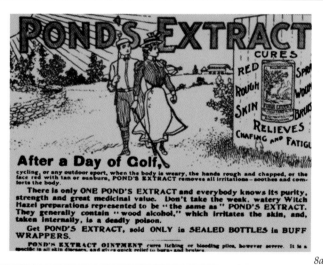

8a

8b

6. *It was not enough to transport your clubs in the back seat or trunk. Better that the world see you are a golfer with the Frisk Auto Caddy that "rides on the running board".*

7. *The Haskell ball patent application, the battle over which was lost in England leading to a series of unwelcome but worthy competitors.*

8. *Nothing was too good for the groundskeepers at Lincoln Park (Illinois) Golf Course, including this "golf ball-proof tractor".*

CRYING ON THE OUTSIDE

"We accept the American invention, as Britons will, of course, with grumbling, but with gratitude down in our hearts."

– Englishman, Horace Hutchinson, in 1903 acknowledging the superiority of the new Haskell golf ball.

STANDARDIZING GOLF BALLS

Coincident with the rumor that a new golf ball with a wonderful flight or carry is to appear this Spring comes the suggestion that golf balls be standardized as baseballs are. The objection raised against the new ball is as follows: Why keep on increasing the length of the links, setting traps at certain distances from the tees, regulating water hazards, and speculating upon natural difficulties when some man can invent a process of making a ball with an extra flight of twenty yards or so that will completely upset the whole scheme of the golf world as exemplified in the courses themselves?

Yard after yard has been added to course after course, until the average high-class links is 6,400 or more yards in length. Will the golfer of the future need the endurance of a camel and the walking qualifications of an Edward Payson Weston?

– New York Times, 1916

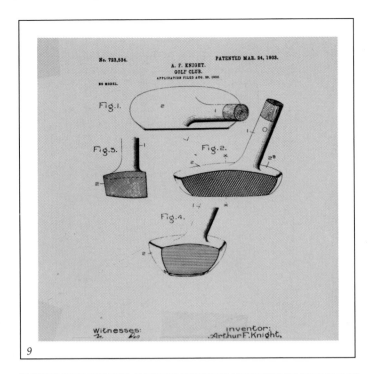

9

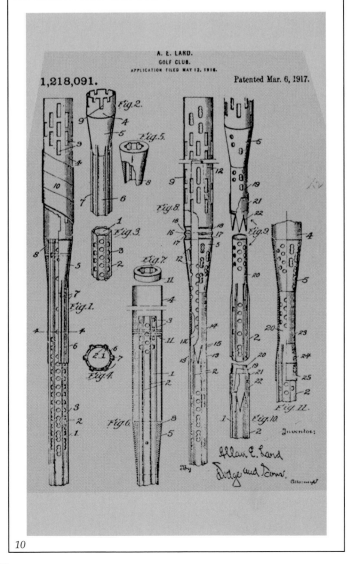

10

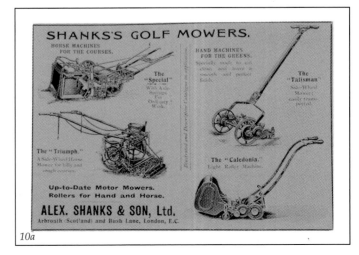

10a

11

9. *The Schenecdaty putter was used successfully for a time by Walter Travis before being banned from professional play for its heretic design. Little matter to Travis who, upon taking up a new putter, said of the Schenecdaty, "I have never been able to do anything with it since. I have tried repeatedly, but it seems to have lost all its virtue."*

10. *Although successfully patented, this perforated steel shaft never gained market acceptance and disappeared.*

11. *MacGregor, a leader in sporting goods as far back as 1925.*

12. *Early clubs and their dashing, if largely forgotten names: (1) putter, (2) cleek – a close faced iron, (3) mashie – today's five iron, (4) driver, (5) short spoon, (6) niblick – pitching wedge, (7) iron putter, (8) long spoon, (9) sand iron, (10) brassie – brass-bottomed two wood.*

DRAWN BY WILL H. DRAKE.
SPECIMENS OF CLUBS.

12

12a

12b

12c

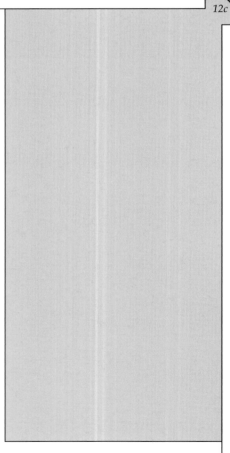

12e

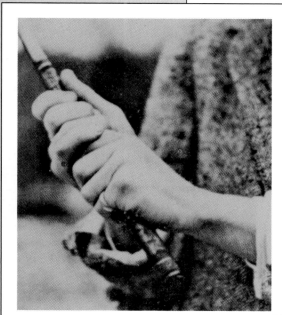

12d

The great Harry Vardon, the British pro known for his many championships and fluid swing. All were attributed to his grip — The Vardon Grip. Envied, emulated, studied and discussed, he described it thus: "Both my hands are practically united by the overlapping of the little finger of the right hand on the index finger of the left hand, with the left thumb straight down the shaft, under the right palm and the right thumb nearly as straight."

13

14

13, 14, & 15. *Stereoscopic photos were once all the rage. Appearing three-dimensional through the handheld viewfinder, a collection of photos provided views of exotic, foreign lands, humorous entertainment ... and golf instructions by popular players of the day. Here Gilbert Nichols demonstrates the use of a sand iron to escape the trap.*

15

16 & 17. "The Old Man", Walter Travis, with the signature cigar clamped sternly in his mouth, lays into one for the pleasure of the home viewing audience.

16

17

WALTER J. TRAVIS.—Driving. Top of swing.

WALTER J. TRAVIS.—Driving. Finish.

18. John J. McDermott, winner of the 1911 and 1912 U.S. Open,
displays an interlocking grip around a thick-shafted mashie.

19. Ed Ray "pitching stymie" to lift his ball over a competitors
in the days before marking balls on the green was legalized, and

20. The finish of a mashie swing.

J. J. McDERMOTT.—Grip. Mashie.

Copyright, by Bay State Publishing Co.

Bay State Publishing Co.
Boston Mass. U.S.A.
London England

431. EDWARD RAY.—Mashie. Finish, right side.

Copyright, by Bay State Publishing Co.

COMPETITIVE GOLF

2. *By 1927 the United States had sealed its world domination of golf with its first Ryder Cup victory over the British. Seated at center is team captain, Walter Hagen, with Gene Serazen at far right.*

COMPETITIVE GOLF

OUIMET WORLD'S GOLF CHAMPION

TWENTY-YEAR-OLD AMATEUR DEFEATS FAMOUS BRITISH PROFESSIONALS FOR OPEN TITLE.

REMARKABLE GOLF FEAT

COVERS THE 18-HOLE COURSE AT BROOKLINE IN 72 STROKES — VARDON 77, RAY 78.

SPLENDID DISPLAY OF NERVE

FIRST AMATEUR TO WIN AMERICAN OPEN CHAMPIONSHIP —BIG GALLERY MAKES DEMONSTRATION AT FINISH.

BROOKLINE, Mass., Sept. 20. — Another name was added to America's list of victors in international sport here today when Francis Ouimet, which for the benefit of the uninitiated is pronounced we-met, a youthful local amateur, won the nineteenth open championship of the United States Golf Association.

The winning of this national title was lifted to an international plane, due to the sensational circumstances of the play and to the calibre of the entrants whom Ouimet defeated during his four-day march to victory. Safely berthed in his qualifying round, the boy trailed the leaders in the first half of the championship round; tied with Harry Vardon and Edward Ray, the famous English professionals, for the first place in the final round, then completely outplayed them today in the eighteen-hole extra round which was necessary to decide the 1913 championship.

Ouimet won with the score of 72 strokes, two under par for one of the hardest courses in the country. Vardon finished five strokes behind Ouimet with 77; Ray took third place with 78.

Ouimet's Rank in Sport.

It was not the actual defeat of this famous pair of golfers so much as the manner of that defeat that entitles Ouimet's name to rank with that of Maurice E. McLoughlin, champion in tennis; Harry Payne Whitney, leader in polo, and James Thorpe, victor in athletics. Ouimet, a tall, slender youth, just past his teens, outplayed and out-nerved not only Vardon and Ray in the play-off, a wonderful fact in itself, but succeeded in battling his way through the largest and most remarkable field of entrants that ever played for an American title. When the qualifying rounds began last Tuesday the lists contained 170 names, including in addition to Vardon and Ray, those of Wilfred Reid, another well-known

1. *The American press and public stood in awe of British golfers. That is, until 1913 when the young American amateur, Francis Ouimet, beat the famed British greats, Harry Vardon and Ted Ray, in the playoff to win the U.S. Open Championship. Ouimet's win generated a new surge of national interest in the game.*

3

3. *The anti-climactic final hole of the 1913 U.S. Open. The great Vardon and Ray were well back of the self-assured young Vardon as he lined up his putt.*

4. *Ouimet on his way to tying Vardon and Ray during the fourth round, forcing the playoff.*

4

6

5

5. *Vardon and Ray, gentlemen to the bitter end, congratulate the upstart Ouimet after his U.S. Open win.*

6. *Ted Ray and Harry Vardon had toured the U.S. winning one match after another. The only question regarding the 1913 U.S. Open seemed to be which one of the two would win it.*

English player; Louis Tellier, a French professional of note; a few high class amateurs, and a host of American and foreign professionals playing for United States and Canadian clubs.

When Ouimet holed his final stroke on the home green of the Country Club this afternoon, the 8,000 persons who had tramped through the heavy mist and dripping grass behind the trio of players for almost three hours realized what the victory meant to American golf, and the scenes of elation which followed were pardonable under the circumstances.

The Winner's Perfect Form.

The pride in the young American's victory was all the more justified because of the fact that he had won without fluke or flaw in his play, responding in perfect form to a test of nerve, stamina and knowledge of golf never before required of a player in a national tournament. All through the crucial journey around the 18-hole course Ouimet never faltered. In fact his play might be termed mechanical, so perfect was it under the trying weather and course conditions. He appeared absolutely without nerve, playing from tee to fairway, from fairway to green and finishing each hole with a splendid exhibition of putting. His veteran opponents, tried players of many a hard-fought match in various parts of the world, broke under the strain, leaving Ouimet to finish as coolly as he had started.

The very fact that Vardon and Ray could not hold up

under the stress of the struggle shows the titanic form and strain of the final round of the championship. Vardon has five times won the English open championship, and in 1900 won the American open at Wheaton, Ill., defeating J.H. Taylor, England's greatest golfer and present champion.

Before the tournament began Ray, Vardon, and Reid were 2 to 1 favorites to win over the remainder of the field. Even after Ouimet had tied with his two opponents of today, wagers were laid at 5 to 4 that one of the two Englishmen would defeat him and even money of Ray or Vardon against Ouimet alone.

The scenes of jubilation on the home green after the match had been won, were, therefore, but natural expressions of pride and pleasure at Ouimet's success in retaining a championship for America which was considered earlier in the week destined to cross the Atlantic.

Ray and Vardon Cheered.

Thousands of dripping rubber-coated spectators massed about Ouimet, who was hoisted to the shoulders of those nearest to him, while cheer after cheer rang out in his honor. Excited women tore bunches of flowers from their bodices and hurled them at the youthful winner; hundreds of men strove to reach him in order to pat him on the back or shake his hand.

Ray and Vardon, whose fight for the open championship brought out the possibilities of Ouimet as

7

10

8

9

The touring British pros who awed the country:

7. *Ted Ray, the power swinger, once said ,"The golfer who has not a friendly feeling for his irons is no gentleman."*

8. *Harry Vardon, the first stylist and pioneer of the overlapping "Vardon grip".*

9. *Vardon (right) first toured the country in 1900 to promote the Vardon Flyer golfball. The rigorous, 20,000 mile tour, which included scores of matches, was a contributor not only to the popularity of the game, but Vardon's serious bout with illness in 1903. He would recover to win two more British Open Championships and lose to Ouimet in the 1913 U.S. contest.*

10. *Ray (putting) and Vardon at right during one of many matches on their American tour.*

a golfer, were not forgotten in the celebration of victory. Each Englishman got a three times three before the parade started for the dressing quarters, where the recent competitors changed to dry clothing for the presentation of the medals and other prizes.

During this ceremony, in which Secretary John Reid, Jr., acted as master of ceremonies, both Ray and Vardon took the opportunity to praise Ouimet as a sportsman and golfer. Ray said the Ouimet had played the best golf during the four-day struggle that he had ever seen in America and that it had been an honor to play with him and no dishonor to lose to him. Vardon brought cheers from the gallery when he frankly stated that they had never had a chance to win with Ouimet, during the play-off, because the lad played better golf and never gave them an opening at one of the eighteen holes. He congratulated Ouimet and America on the victory and proved a popular speechmaker as well as golfer. Secretary Reid, in awarding the championship medal to Ouimet, the trophy to the Woodland Club of Auburndale, Mass., which he represented, and cash prizes to Vardon and Ray, took occasion to apologize "in a slight way" as he put it, for the outbursts of cheering at inopportune times.

This was a delicate reference to a feature of today's play which is quite likely to be a subject of international

11

13.—JEROME D. TRAVERS; with Havemeyer Cup, American Amateur Championship Trophy.

11. *Jerome Travers, one of America's great competitive golfers, with the U.S. Amateur Championship trophy which he won in 1907, 1908, 1912 and 1913 along with the U.S. Open in 1915.*

He derided the stylist zealots in 1924 when he wrote, "I believe that many of us here (in the U.S.) are prone to take the game too seriously, which doesn't help in the slightest to mold the proper mental attitude towards it. For another, we have a tendency to be too deliberate. That is a real handicap. Step on any golf course and watch the average American golfer as he fiddles around before swinging his club ... I am convinced that the average player would get more enjoyment and better scores if he abandoned the national habit of overemphasizing the care necessary in every shot."

Following spread 12. "Final round for Stickney Cup, Graham driving, Mount Pleasant Golf Links, White Mountains", circa 1890 - 1901. "Graham" could be the fine British amateur, John Graham, killed during WW I.

13

comment by the golfing contingents of England and the United States. The management of the tournament has been the subject of much praise, but today the gallery several times violated the keen ethics of the sport, by cheering wildly whenever Ouimet gained a point. The same outbursts occurred yesterday, but Ouimet was then playing with George Sargent, who had no chance for first place in the final half of his round. Today it was different, for both Ray and Vardon were playing shots either just before or after Ouimet and it was plainly evident that these outbreaks annoyed them. Approaching the seventeenth hole, Ray deliberately stopped in the midst of a swing and refused to play until the cheering ceased. This action of the gallery had little or no effect on the result of the match, but a number of golfers publicly voiced their regret that cheering like that at boat races or football games should have occurred, although they realized and stated that it was impossible to check these national outbursts of enthusiasm when Ouimet made particularly good plays.

How the Strokes Were Made.

It was exactly 10 o'clock when the trio of players teed up in the drizzle for the start. The fairways and

14

15

13 & 14. Some of the gallery at Essex Country Club, circa 1900 and at Baltusrol, New Jersey, 1908.

15. Walter Travis, U.S. Amateur Champ of 1900, 1901 and 1903, sends one screaming off the tee. Ironically during this period, amateur players were generally superior to most pros.

16

17

18

16. *U.S. Open Champ of 1908 and USPGA Champ of 1919, Fred McLeod, with Alex "miss 'em quick" Smith.*

17. *"Miss 'em quick" Smith, known not so much for his trophies (although he won the 1906 and 1910 U.S. Opens), but for his quick putting.*

18. *Mike Brady, with no championships of record, was runner-up "to the best of 'em" losing the 1911 U.S. Open Championship playoff to J.J. McDermott and again in 1919, the same championship, again a playoff, losing to Walter Hagen.*

greens were water-soaked and in many places churned to the consistency of muddy paste by the trampling of hundreds of feet during the last three days of rain. Overhead low-hanging gray clouds appeared to be part of the mist which would have made the most ardent Scotch golfer feel perfectly at home. The first and second holes were recorded in fives and fours for all three players.

Both Ray and Vardon outdrove Ouimet from the tees, but both sliced and pulled slightly, while the ultimate winner held true to the course.

The first break came at the third hole, where Ray took a five, while the other two players holed in four. There was no advantage either way on the fourth and fifth, but Vardon took the lead in the sixth with a three, while Ray and Ouimet required four. Ray drove furthest, but Vardon's approach was right on the green and he holed a comparatively easy putt, while Ray and Ouimet needed two.

Vardon and Ouimet took four for the short seventh, approaching indifferently, while Ray was on the green in two and holed a brilliant putt for three, drawing up even with Ouimet. Vardon lost his lead in the eighth, when, after getting on the green in two, he putted badly, requiring two to hole. Ouimet's second was within a foot of the pin, and he scored an easy three. Ray arose to the occasion with a beautiful 25-foot putt for a three also. All took fives on the ninth, the longest and hardest hole of the course, being 520 yards of hill and dale, known as the Himalayas.

It therefore came about that the two Englishmen and the American youth played the greatest match in the history of golf on this continent, turning for home all square at 38.

Ouimet immediately jumped to the fore with a three on the short tenth. All were on the green in one, but Ray and Vardon each needed three putts to hole, while Ouimet from his more favorable lie, scored with two. This gave him a lead of a stroke and marked the beginning of the end.

The eleventh was halved in four, but Ouimet picked up another stroke on the twelfth. He outdrove both opponents from the tee and his approach was within eight feet of the hole, but he took two putts for a four. Ray and Vardon both had trouble in getting to the edge of the green in twos, and, putting poorly, halved in five. All landed on the thirteenth green with their second shots, but Vardon's perfect putt gave him a three, while Ouimet and Ray took two for fours.

The fourteenth was halved in five, and with but four holes to play Ouimet was leading by the narrow margin of one stroke. Vardon stayed with him on the fifteenth, each getting a four, but Ray, after hitting a spectator with

his sliced drive, reached the sand trap on the mashie shot. He required two to get on the green and two putts for a six. He was now four strokes behind Ouimet and three behind Vardon, and his experience appeared to break his playing nerve.

On the sixteenth, the shortest hole of the course, all played the 125-yard iron shot to the green. Vardon and Ouimet made par threes, but Ray required three putts for a four, so off was he on his game.

Ouimet won the match and title on the seventeenth, when he got a three for his opponents' fives. The youngster drove far down the fairway, was on the green in two, and holed a short putt, one stroke below par. Vardon, who had been showing signs of the strain, hooked his drive in to a trap, took three to the green, and two putts to hole. Ray was in deep grass, and, playing as though he had given up hope, halved the hole with his countryman. He rallied and scored a three on the home hole with a long putt, while Ouimet, playing safe, had a par four. Vardon's second shot was short, landing in the mud of the race course, and when he finally holed for the last time of the match, his card showed a six.

A resume of the play shows that while Ouimet was frequently outdriven with iron and wood, his game was far steadier and more consistent than that of either Ray or Vardon. The two Englishmen showed a tendency to slice and pull their first and second shots, which got them into trouble frequently. While Ouimet did not get the distance of his competitors, he played line shots all during the match, his direction being little short of remarkable, considering the soft, muddy condition of the turf. In putting, too, he was steadier and more accurate than either Ray or Vardon.

– New York Times, 1913

DEGRADING GOLF

The managers of the famous Country Club at Brookline, Mass., will do themselves and their club injustice if they fail to take action of some sort in regard to the rowdyism which has lately disgraced the ancient and honorable game of golf on their course. The circumstances thus far, of course, reflect no sort of discredit on the Brookline club, for everybody knows that no member of that organization of well-bred men would demean himself by a show of favoritism while following a golf match. Cheers and cries of encouragement or the reverse are wholly out of place in the game of golf. As a matter of fact that game does not lend itself easily to exhibition purposes. However, when spectators are permitted to follow a match they should be

19. Nor were the U.S. ladies averse to tournament play. One of the renowned woman golfers, Glenna Collett receives the U.S. Women's U.S. Golf Championship trophy as runner-up Virginia Van Wie stands by.

20. Collett (Mrs. Edwin H. Vare) lost the 1931 championship to "hard-hitting" Helen Hicks, putting here on the 18th hole. The loss prevented Collett from winning the title a record fourth-straight time.

held strictly to the rules. Not a word should be spoken during the play, and no expression of approval or disapproval should be permitted at any time.

Mr. Jerome Travers was insulted at Brookline Friday, as Vardon and Ray, the two English professionals, had previously been insulted by the crowd of irresponsible sightseers permitted to walk over the course. Certainly a golfer like Mr. Ouimet should be among the first to discountenance a manifestation of this sort in his favor, though Mr. Travers, like Vardon and Ray, may regard it as beneath notice. Golf is peculiarly a nervous game; many players who do very well in club matches under ordinary conditions "go to pieces" when spectators follow them. In the history of golf in Great Britain there have been no manifestations of gross ill-breeding comparable with those recently seen at Brookline. The fault is not with that club, as we have said, but an expression of disapproval of the ill-bred cheering from the Brookline Governors would be appropriate and would go far to prevent such vulgar exhibitions in the future.

– New York Times, 1913

19

20

Walter Hagen Wins Open Golf Title

Walter C. Hagen, 22 years old, native professional of Rochester, N.Y., today displaced Francis Ouimet as open golf champion of America, by winning the tournament at Midlothian with a medal score of 290 for the seventy-two holes.

Hagen's victory was accomplished by steady playing. Yesterday he made a record of 68 for the course by good work, aided by spectacular putting. He took 74 in the afternoon, leading the field at the end of the first day with 142. Today he fell off a trifle, taking 75 for the first round and 73 for the second. The best of his game came on the last nine holes, where, holing putt after putt, he made 35, two under par.

The new champion was born in Rochester, learned golf there and had not made any record outside his native city until the present tournament. He is slight in build, but follows Vardon's system of shooting straight for the flag all the time.

Golf Great

The national open championship of 1916 is a thing of the past, and on the pinnacle of golf in this country stands a figure that is attracting the admiring wonder of golf enthusiasts for at least four good reasons. Chick Evans is young, and that in itself is attractive; he earned the title by the skill of his hands and the courage of his heart, and that makes it a matter of justice; he is an amateur, and by this token he is the idol of thousands of those who love the game for what there is in it, not for what they can get out of it; he is an American, and throughout the country has swept a feeling of pride that a homebred youngster has been able to defeat those who, only a few short years ago, came to these shores to teach us how to play the game – the Englishmen whose golf is their lifework, the Scotchmen whose golf is their religion!

– New York Times

21

21. *"Miss E. Pickhardt" swings for the camera.*

22. *British golf professionals posed an equal threat to U.S. ladies as to the men. Here England's Women's Golf Champ rings the all clear with her club as she heads for the seventh hole. She captained the women's team that turned back the lady invaders from the states.*

THE "HAG" SPEAKS

"I don't want to be a millionaire. I just want to live like one."
– Walter Hagen

GEORGIA'S GOLF MARVEL

According to reports from Georgia there is a 13-year-old golfer in that part of the country who will soon give Chick Evans and Jerry Travers cause to look to their laurels. The boy is Bob Jones of the East Lake Country Club at Atlanta. Thomas B. Paine, Chairman of the House Committee of the club, is sponsor for a card of 68 that the youngster turned in for the 6,464 - yard links of the home club. This ties the professional record for the course made by Stewart Maiden, a brother of Jimmie Maiden of Nassau, who is the professional in charge of the links.

Par for the long course is 73, and as he exceeded par by a stroke on two holes, he was required to beat par by a stroke on seven other holes. On the journey to the turn he got the 320-yard par 4 third hole in 3, the 440-yard

22

23

24

25

23. *Jerome Travers is carried to the club house at Baltrusol after his 1915 U.S. Open win.*

24. *A beaming Travers holds up his U.S. Open trophy.*

25. *The flamboyant, audacious, arrogant Walter Hagen first broke onto the scene in 1913 when he placed fourth behind Ouimet, Vardon and Ray in the U.S. Open. A fashion trend-setter, he was also the greatest international golfer from the late 1900's through the 1920's. Powerful but erratic off the tee, he was renowned for his remarkable recoveries when on the course and his escapades when off. He once showed up at the start of a tournament wearing his rumpled tuxedo of the night before. "Hagen's in golf to live," Chick Evans once said of him, "not to make a living." Nonetheless, the "Hag" became golf's first million dollar career winner.*

pare 5 fourth hole in 4, and the 230-yard par 4 eighth hole in 3, completing his outward journey in 34 strokes, three under par. He lost a stroke on the first hole coming in, but a 3 on the 380-yard par 4 twelfth hole brought him even again. On the 400-yard thirteenth he took another 3, but lost the advantage by getting a 6 on teh 450-yard fourteenth. A 4 on the 480-yard fifteenth and a 2 on the 190-yard home hole gave him 34 strokes or his inward journey and a 68 for the entire round. His card follows:

Out............4   3   3   4   5   3   4   3   5 - 34
In..............5   3   3   3   6   4   4   4   2 - 34 – GS

Last year when only 12 years old the boy won the championship of the Roebuck Springs Golf Club, an invitation tournament at Birmingham, Ala., the championship of the East Lake Country Club at Atlanta, the championship of the Druid Hills Country Club, and set new amateur records for the two last-named links.
– New York Times, 1916

GRIT

"My God, I don't think I can finish."
– Ben Hogan, still recovering from injuries sustained in an auto accident, during the fourth round of the 1950 U.S. Open. He rallied to win in a grueling play off.

27

28

27. Robert Tyre Jones, better known as "The Immortal Bobby Jones", still quite likely the greatest golfer to ever play the game. Although retiring from competitive golf at the age of 28, he left behind this record: U.S. Amateur Champion, 1924, 1925, 1927, 1928, 1930; U.S. Open Champion, 1923, 1926, 1930; British Open Champion, 1926, 1927, 1930; British Amateur Champion, 1930.

28. Jones sinks the 45-foot putt that won him the U.S. Open four-times running at the Interlachen Golf Club, Minneapolis.

29. Beloved throughout the world, but particularly at St. Andrews, Scotland, where the 10th hole is named after him, and in the United States where in 1930 he was honored by a New York ticker tape parade after winning the Grand Slam; the American and British Open and Amateur Championships - a herculean feat.

29